Going Places

Mexico

Cari Meister

ABDO Publishing Company

visit us at
www.abdopub.com

Published by ABDO Publishing Company 4940 Viking Drive, Edina, Minnesota 55435.
Copyright © 2000 by Abdo Consulting Group, Inc. International copyrights reserved in all countries. No part of this book may be reproduced in any form without written permission from the publisher.

Printed in the United States.

Photo credits: AP/Wide World, Peter Arnold, Inc.

Edited by Lori Kinstad Pupeza
Contributing editors Morgan Hughes, Carmen Pereda
Graphic designs by Linda O'Leary

Library of Congress Cataloging-in-Publication Data

Meister, Cari.
    Mexico / Cari Meister.
    p. cm. -- (Going places)
    Includes index.
    Summary: Describes a variety of tourist attractions in Mexico including Teotihuacán, Mayan ruins, Aztec artifacts, markets and plazas in Mexico City, and areas of Baja California and Acapulco.
    ISBN 1-57765-029-8
    1. Mexico--Juvenile literature. [1. Mexico.] I. Title. II. Series: Meister, Cari. Going places.
    F1208.5.M45   2000
    972--dc21
                                            98-10131
                                            CIP
                                            AC

Contents

Visiting Mexico

Mexico is a great country to visit. You can play on the beautiful beaches. You can watch Mexican dancers. You can explore the biggest city in the world.

You can also brush up on your Spanish. More people speak Spanish in Mexico than anywhere else in the world. Mexicans speak Spanish because Mexico was once ruled by Spain.

Some Mexicans speak Native American languages. There are over 50 groups of Native Americans, and over 50 kinds of their languages. They have lived in Mexico for thousands of years, long before the Spanish came.

Exploring Mexico is fun.

Many things in Mexico are a mix of Spanish and Native American: buildings, fiestas, clothing, food, and people. Mexicans are proud of their mixed background. Today, most Mexicans are **Mestizos**.

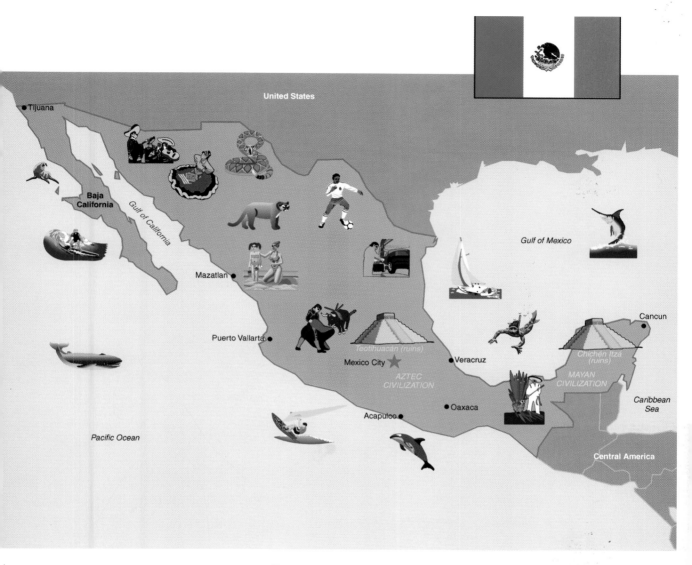

United States

Tijuana

Baja
California

Gulf of California

Mazatlan

Puerto Vallarta

Pacific Ocean

Acapulco

Teotihuacan (ruins)

Mexico City

AZTEC
CIVILIZATION

Oaxaca

Gulf of Mexico

Veracruz

Cancun

Chichén Itzá
(ruins)

MAYAN
CIVILIZATION

Caribbean
Sea

Central America

An illustrated map of Mexico.

Teotihuacán

*P*ut on your hiking boots. Get out your camera. You won't want to miss anything at Teotihuacán (tay-o-tee-wah-KAN).

More than 2,000 years ago Teotihuacán was a thriving city of more than 200,000 people. Nobody lives in Teotihuacán anymore. In about 300 A.D., the city was destroyed by a fire. Today, the ancient city is a popular **tourist** spot. It is located just north of Mexico City.

The Teotihuacáns built huge pyramids. They also built a Pyramid of the Sun as well as a Pyramid of the Moon. You can hike up both pyramids. When you are at the top of the Pyramid of the Moon, you can see a road. The road, named Quetzalcóatl (ket-sahl-KO-ah-tl), is called the Avenue of the Dead.

The Avenue of the Dead leads to the Temple of Quetzalcóatl. The temple was built in honor of an Aztec god. The Teotihuacáns believed the god Quetzalcóatl brought peace to their city. Quetzalcóatl is represented by a serpent. Look for pictures of him on the side of the temple.

The Pyramid of the Sun at Teotihuacán.

Mayan Ruins

*A*round the same time that Teotihuacán was built, the Maya were building great pyramids. They knew a lot about the sun and stars. They created the best calendar of the time.

The Maya lived further south than the Teotihuacáns. The Maya lived in the part of Mexico known as Yucatán. They also lived in Central America. There are many places you can see Mayan **ruins** in Mexico.

One place you can visit is Chichén Itzá (chee-CHEN eet-ZAH). There are hundreds of buildings at Chichén Itzá. About 20 to 30 buildings are open to visitors. You can explore ball courts, temples, and **sacred** wells.

The tallest building is called El Castillo. El Castillo means "The Castle." There are 365 steps on The Castle, one for each day of the year. Two times a year there are special light and shadow shows at The Castle.

El Castillo at Chichén Itzá, Mexico.

The Aztecs

*T*he Aztecs were powerful warriors. They lived in Mexico before the Spanish arrived. They do not date back as far as the Maya or the Teotihuacáns. The Aztecs settled about 700 years ago.

The Aztecs ruled over many different tribes. They ruled from a strong city. The city, called Tenochtitlán, was built on an island. Canoes were used to travel back and forth to the mainland.

Tenochtitlán was destroyed by Spanish explorers. The explorers discovered Mexico in 1517. They wanted to have cities there for Spanish people to live in. The Aztecs tried to keep them from building cities, but they could not.

The Spanish built Mexico City over the Aztec **ruins**. Today, there is no longer an island. The water between the island and the mainland soaked into the earth.

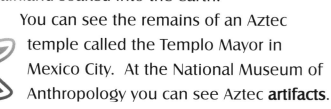

You can see the remains of an Aztec temple called the Templo Mayor in Mexico City. At the National Museum of Anthropology you can see Aztec **artifacts**.

*This photo shows an archaeological excavation
of an aztec site in Mexico City.*

Exploring Mexico City

*M*exico City, Mexico's capital, is the most populated city in the world. Over 20 million people live there.

There are many places to visit in the city. The **zócalo** is in the city's center. A zócalo is a central plaza. People gather in the zócalo to shop, watch festivals, and visit with friends.

Close to the zócalo is an outdoor market. Count your **pesos**. You will see belts, blankets, and other Mexican items for sale. Most large cities in Mexico have a zócalo.

At the Plaza de Toros, you can watch a **bullfight**. Bullfighting is a very popular sport in Mexico. If you want to see a bullfight, go on Sunday. There are more bullfights on Sunday than on any other day. The music and costumes will make you feel like you stepped back in time.

At the Palacio de Bellas Artes, the Baile Folklórico (BA-ee-lay fohl-LOHR-ee-coh) dances. These dances tell stories of long ago.

The Central Library of the National Autonomous University of Mexico in Mexico City.

Exploring Baja California

*B*aja California is the narrow strip of land that extends south from the California, or United States border. The Gulf of California separates Baja California from the rest of Mexico.

If you enjoy exploring the ocean, Baja California is a place for you. Many visitors come to Baja California to see ocean animals. There are special tour guides that take families on **expeditions**. There are expeditions on land. There are also boat expeditions.

Many visitors go on the Laguna San Ignacio Gray Whale Adventure. Here, you sleep in tents in the desert. During the day, boats take you out into the ocean. Watch the waters. You will see gray whales. Gray whales do not scare easily. They are sometimes called "the friendly whales."

Another adventure takes you to Magdalena Bay. Magdalena Bay is calmer than Laguna San Ignacio. There are not very many waves. Magdalena Bay is perfect for people who are afraid of getting seasick.

Cabo San Lucas, Baja California.

Exploring Acapulco

*M*any people from all over the world visit Acapulco to bask in the sun. Others go to Acapulco to play in the water. Acapulco is located on the southwestern side of Mexico.

Acapulco is usually very warm and sunny. There are many beaches to visit. Most of the city sits along the bay. Visitors spend their time **snorkeling**, swimming, and exploring the beaches.

There are other things to do, too. Many people enjoy walking around the mercado, or market. Other people enjoy tasting cabrito al pastor (roasted goat) and local **tamales**.

Acapulco has many fine museums and **aquariums**. At Mágico Mundo Marino you can see sea turtles, tropical fish, and dolphins.

Be sure not to miss the cliff divers! Cliff divers jump from cliffs into the ocean. Some of the cliffs are 130 feet (40 m) high. Acapulco cliff divers jump with burning torches at night.

Beachfront in Acapulco, Mexico.

Mexican Fiestas

Mexicans have many celebrations called fiestas. Mexicans make special foods and decorations for fiestas.

You will see piñatas in the markets all over Mexico. Kids celebrate their birthdays with piñatas. A piñata is a colorful decoration made of special paper. A piñata is usually in the shape of an animal or bird. Candy, small toys, and coins are hidden inside the piñata.

At a fiesta, kids are blindfolded. They take turns hitting the piñata with a stick. Finally, someone makes a crack in the piñata and the treats fall to the ground.

If you are lucky enough to visit Mexico on November 2 you will see Mexicans celebrate **El Día de los Muertos**. El Día de los Muertos means "The Day of the Dead."

The Day of the Dead is the day the living honor the dead. There are special breads to eat. Some of the breads are shaped like skeletons. People stay up all night. Families picnic in graveyards.

A young boy laughs while swinging at a piñata during a fiesta. The festival features Mexican food, music, and traditional art and craft work.

Traveling in Mexico

*T*raveling in Mexico is a lot of fun. There are many things to see and do.

Do not forget that you are traveling in a **foreign** country. Some things about Mexico are very different from home. Keep the following things in mind:

• Drink bottled water. In the United States, water is tested to make sure it is okay to drink. Not all of the water in Mexico has been tested. You can get very sick from drinking untested water.

• Do not eat large portions of food. Mexicans cook with things that you may not be used to. Your body may have a hard time digesting some of the food.

• Always carry identification. You will need to prove you are from the United States.

• Wear sunscreen. The sun is very bright in Mexico. If you burn, you will be miserable.

Bikers tour Playa del Carmen on the Yucatán Peninsula, Mexico.

Glossary

Artifacts: objects made by humans remaining from another time or culture.

Aquariums: man-made containers for fish and sea animals.

Bullfighting: a sport in which a person fights a bull in an arena.

El Día de los Muertos: a Mexican celebration where the living honor the dead.

Expeditions: adventurous travel vacations.

Foreign: a different country, not your own.

Mestizos: Mexicans that have both Spanish and Native American ancestors.

Pesos: Mexican money.

Ruins: the remains of something destroyed.

Sacred: holy, very special.

Snorkeling: an underwater activity that uses a breathing tube and mask.

Tamales: ground meat and spices wrapped in cornmeal dough and corn husks then steamed.

Tourist: a person who travels to visit a place for fun.

Zócalo: central plaza.

Internet Sites

Canadian CultureNet
http://www.culturenet.ucalgary.ca/
CultureNet is a World Wide Web window on Canadian culture. It is a home for Canadian cultural networks.

The Disney World Explorer
http://www.disney.com/DisneyInteractive/WDWExplorer/
This is a fun and colorful site with trivia games, maps, previews, downloads, CD-ROM helpers and much, much more.

Grand Canyon Association
http://www.thecanyon.com/gca/
You're just a click away from a backpacking trip, a chance to meet canyon lovers like you, and books on this great region. This site has some great artwork.

Mexconnect
http://www.mexconnect.com/
This site has great travel ideas, Mexican art, tradition, food, history, and much more. It includes a chat room, tour section, and photo gallery.

Fantastic Journeys Yellowstone
http://www.nationalgeographic.com/features/97/yellowstone/index.html
Explore Yellowstone National Park, a place like no other on Earth. See strange marvels, go underground to find what causes them, and trigger an eruption of the famous geyser Old Faithful. A very cool site!

Marine Watch
http://www.marinewatch.com/
Welcome to Marine Watch, the international news journal about events occurring on, under and over the oceans of the planet. This site has many links and cool photos!

These sites are subject to change.

Pass It On

Adventure Enthusiasts: Tell us about places you've been or want to see. A national park, amusement park, or any exciting place you want to tell us about. We want to hear from you!

To get posted on the ABDO Publishing Company website E-mail us at
"Adventure@abdopub.com"
Visit the ABDO Publishing Company website at www.abdopub.com

Index